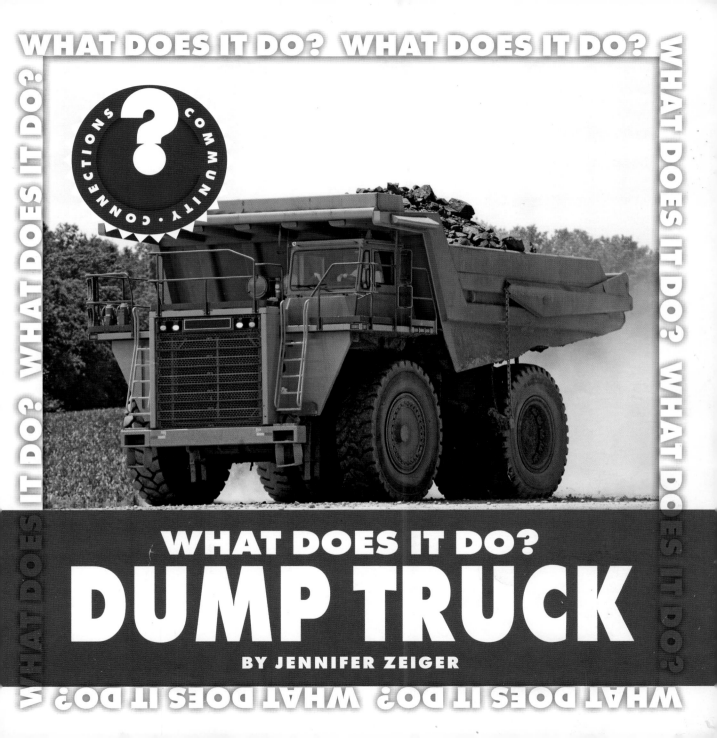

COMMUNITY · CONNECTIONS

?

WHAT DOES IT DO?

DUMP TRUCK

BY JENNIFER ZEIGER

CHERRY LAKE
Publishing

Published in the United States of America by Cherry Lake Publishing
Ann Arbor, Michigan
www.cherrylakepublishing.com

Content Adviser: Louis Teel, Professor of Heavy Equipment, Central Arizona College
Reading Adviser: Cecilia Minden-Cupp, PhD, Literacy Consultant

Photo Credits: Cover and page 1, ©iStockphoto.com/romanbaechtold; page 5, ©Robert J.
Beyers II/Shutterstock, Inc.; page 7, ©Howard Sandler/Shutterstock, Inc.; page 9,
©mashe/Shutterstock, Inc.; page 11, ©Robert Pernell/Shutterstock, Inc.; page 13, ©Robert
Asento/Shutterstock, Inc.; page 15, ©Ivaschenko Roman/Shutterstock, Inc.; page 17,
©Baloncici/Shutterstock, Inc.; page 19, ©Emily Riddell/Alamy; page 21, ©Frank Jr/
Shutterstock, Inc.

LIBRARY OF CONGRESS CATALOGING-IN-PUBLICATION DATA
Zeiger, Jennifer.
 What does it do? Dump truck/by Jennifer Zeiger.
    p. cm.—(Community connections)
 Includes bibliographical references and index.
 ISBN-13: 978-1-60279-974-5 (lib. bdg.)
 ISBN-10: 1-60279-974-1 (lib. bdg.)
 1. Dump trucks—Juvenile literature. I. Title. II. Title: Dump truck. III. Series.
 TL230.15.Z45 2011
 629.225—dc22   2010023584

Cherry Lake Publishing would like to acknowledge the
work of The Partnership for 21st Century Skills. Please
visit www.21stcenturyskills.org for more information.

Printed in the United States of America
Corporate Graphics Inc.
January 2011
CLSP08

DUMP TRUCK

CONTENTS

WHAT DOES IT DO?

HEAVY DUTY

A big truck drives up to a pile of dirt. A power shovel scoops up the dirt. It dumps the dirt into the back of the truck. The truck carries the full **load** away. It will soon come back for more.

What is this hardworking machine? It's a dump truck!

A power shovel fills the back of a dump truck.

Dump trucks are built to carry heavy loads. Many can carry 50 tons or more. Fifty tons is the weight of about nine elephants!

These big trucks can carry almost anything. Their engines are powerful enough to move heavy loads.

Some dump trucks are used to help clear snow from roads.

The **cab** is at the front of the truck. This is where the driver sits.

The dump box is just behind the cab. This is where loads are carried. Sometimes a dump box has a **tailgate** at the back. The tailgate opens so the dump box can be emptied.

Dump trucks have large wheels.

Look carefully at this dump truck. Can you name some of its parts? How many wheels do you see? Can you spot the steps the driver uses to reach the cab?

CLEARING OUT, BRINGING IN

One job a dump truck can do is help clean up. **Mining** and building stir up rocks and dirt. Dump trucks carry these away.

Dump trucks are helpful at mines. They carry away coal, copper, or other things that are dug from the earth.

Dump trucks can carry loads for many miles.

Construction sites often need extra sand or gravel. Dump trucks ⸻ these things to the site. ⸻ trucks can pour ⸻ or fix roads. ⸻ lt on icy ⸻ Then

13

SPECIAL TRUCKS

Most dump boxes **tilt** up and down. This empties the load from the back of the box.

Some boxes dump to the side. They can be emptied faster than other dump boxes.

Other dump boxes empty out of the bottom. They can spread gravel or other materials.

This dump box tilts up. Do you see the tailgate?

THINK!

Dump trucks don't work alone. Think about a work site. What jobs need to be done? Which machines help dump trucks? Which machines take over after a dump truck has done its job?

Dump trucks come in all sizes. Some are very small. Some are very big. Mini dump trucks carry smaller loads. They are sometimes used on farms. The biggest dump trucks can carry the weight of 115 cars or more!

You might see a truck with a small dump basket at your local park.

New **technology** helps make dump trucks better. Many dump trucks include a special computer system. It keeps track of what the truck does. It can tell when a part needs to be fixed. This keeps the truck working.

This giant dump truck can be seen in Canada.

SPARWOOD B.C.

19

Dump trucks do their part to get the job done. They make many tasks faster and easier to do. Dump trucks are important machines!

It usually takes more than one machine to do a big job.

GLOSSARY

asphalt (ASS-fawlt) a thick, black material used to pave roads

cab (KAB) the part of a large truck or machine where the driver or operator sits

construction sites (kuhn-STRUK-shuhn SITESS) areas where something is being built

load (LOHD) something that is carried

mining (MINE-ing) digging up minerals that are found underground

tailgate (TALE-gayt) a gate at the back of a truck that can be lifted or folded down

technology (tek-NOL-uh-jee) inventions that help people do things

tilt (TILT) to tip or slant to one side

FIND OUT MORE

BOOKS

Graham, Ian. *Dump Trucks and Other Big Machines*. Irvine, CA: QEB, 2008.

Oxlade, Chris. *This Is My Dump Truck*. North Mankato, MN: Sea to Sea, 2007.

Tourville, Amanda Doering. *Dump Trucks*. Edina, MN: Magic Wagon, 2009.

WEB SITES

DLTK's Crafts for Kids: Egg Carton Dump Truck
www.dltk-kids.com/crafts/transportation/megg_carton_dump_truck.htm
Learn how to make your own toy dump truck.

Kikki's Workshop
www.kenkenkikki.jp/e_index.html
This site has pictures, activities, and a lot of information about dump trucks and other big machines.

INDEX

ABOUT THE AUTHOR

Jennifer Zeiger
is a graduate of
DePaul University.
She studied English,
though she loves to
learn about nearly
anything. She lives in
the Chicago area.

24